Other books by Ben Okri:

Fiction

Flowers and Shadows
The Landscapes Within
Incidents at the Shrine
Stars of the New Curfew
The Famished Road
Songs of Enchantment
Astonishing the Gods
Dangerous Love
Infinite Riches
In Arcadia
Starbook
Tales of Freedom

Non-Fiction

Birds of Heaven
A Way of Being Free

Poetry

An African Elegy
Mental Fight

A TIME FOR NEW DREAMS

POETIC ESSAYS

BEN OKRI

RIDER

LONDON · SYDNEY · AUCKLAND · JOHANNESBURG

1 3 5 7 9 10 8 6 4 2

Published in 2011 by Rider, an imprint of Ebury Publishing
Ebury Publishing is a Random House Group company

The Random House Group Limited Reg. No. 954009

Addresses for companies within the Random House Group can be found at
www.randomhouse.co.uk

A CIP catalogue record for this book is available from the British Library

The Random House Group Limited supports The Forest Stewardship
Council (FSC), the leading international forest certification organisation.
All our titles that are printed on Greenpeace approved FSC certified paper
carry the FSC logo. Our paper procurement policy can be found at
www.randomhouse.co.uk/environment

Mixed Sources
Product group from well-managed
forests and other controlled sources
www.fsc.org   Cert no. TT-COC-2139
© 1996 Forest Stewardship Council

Printed and bound in Great Britain by CPI Mackays, Chatham ME5 8TD

ISBN 9781846042683

To Paul Marsh

CONTENTS

And out of the wilderness
The songbird sang . . .

POETRY AND LIFE

1

Heaven knows we need poetry now more than ever. We need the awkward truth of poetry. We need its indirect insistence on the magic of listening.

In a world of contending guns, the argument of bombs, and the madness of believing that only our side, our religion, our politics is right, a world fatally inclined towards war – we need the voice that speaks to the highest in us.

We need the voice that speaks to our joys, our childhoods, and to the Gordian knots of our private and national condition. A voice that speaks to our doubts, our fears, and to all the unsuspected dimensions that make us both human and beings touched by the whisperings of the stars.

2

Poetry is closer to us than politics, and is as intrinsic to us as walking or eating.

We are, at birth, born into a condition of poetry and breathing. Birth is a poetic condition: it is spirit becoming flesh. Death is also a poetic condition: it is flesh becoming spirit again. It is the miracle of a circle completed, the unheard melody of a life returning to unmeasured silence.

Between birth and death what are our daily moments but a double condition that is primarily poetic: the odd conjunction between inner and outer, between that inner sense of timelessness and that outer evidence of transience?

3

Statesmen talk about matters of state; poets help us to resonate with the fundamental rhythm of life, the iambics of walking, the elliptical strophes of every unique way of talking, the mysterious pulse of living.

Poetry begins in us an inner dialogue. It suggests a private journey to one's own truth.

Let us bring together the voices of poetry from all over the world, and make our hearts a festival, a dreaming place, and our minds an academy of essentials under the stars.

4

Poetry is not just what poets write. Poetry is also the great river of soul-murmurings that runs within humanity. Poets merely bring this underground river to the surface for a moment, here and there, in cascades of sound and suggested meaning, through significant form.

5

The ancient oracles may be silent; and we may no longer believe in the many ways that the gods speak to us, or through us. But living means that we are the focus of many pressures: the demands of society, the strange pressures of being itself, of yearnings, inexplicable moods, dreams, and of feelings powerful with all the currents of mortal life.

6

We concentrate too much on our differences. Poetry returns us to the surprise of our similarities. It brings us back to the obscure sense that we are all members of a far-flung family, sharing feelings both unique to us and oddly universal.

We need more poetry than politics. But we need to constantly raise the possibilities of poetry. Poetry will not necessarily change the world. (Tyrants have been known to be poets, that is to say bad poets.) But so long as poetry sends our minds into realms of gold and questions, and touches our deep and tender humanity, then it will always be a force for beauty, for good, in the world, neutralising slowly the noise of guns and hatred.

7

The reason for the exalted condition of poetry is simple. Poetry is a descendant of the original word which mystics believe gave the impulse for all creation.

Poetry, at its highest, has alive in it, even in homeopathic doses, the creative power of the universe. Poetry incarnates that which shapes, changes, transforms. It makes something from what seems like nothing. How insubstantial words are! Who can weigh a word on a scale, even against a feather of truth? And yet see how much words weigh in the heart, in the imagination, in dreams, echoing down the ages, as durable as the Pyramids. Words, lighter than air, are as mysteriously enduring as lived time. Poetry hints at the godlike in us, and causes us to resonate with high places of being.

8

Poets want nothing from you, only that you listen to your deepest selves. Unlike politicians, they don't want your votes.

True poets just want you to honour the original pact you made with the universe when you drew your first breath from the unseen magic in the air.

On Childhood (1)

1

Childhood is a mystery: the soul is timeless, the body new, and the world complex. What a conjunction: the great unfolding in the small. This is why childhood fascinates us. It is elusive. It is elusive in us.

Our childhood has disappeared in our ageing. Memories linger, perceptions remain, but the state itself is gone. Gone also is its world.

And childhood is a world, a separate realm. Its wondrous angles can't be relived. Its confusions are dissolved into wrong certainties. Its terrors still lurk in us, but we can't exactly locate them.

We are left with observing the childhood of others. We gaze into them as into a mirror. As if childhood were generic. When in fact childhood is specific to the child.

And so when we peer into childhood's mirror we see only dim reflections. Vague memories of a lost world rise in us. But we are not invited back. The borders are closed. The realm in the mirror has vanished from the world. We are thus exiled in adulthood: either closed to, or perplexed by, mysteries.

2

Childhood evokes only nostalgia, when it should also evoke unease. For childhood is a philosophical problem always posed to living. The state of childhood asks questions that are seldom answered.

Childhood asks us what reality really is, what the world is, and where it came from. Childhood asks where life came from, and where it goes. Does the soul exist? Where was the soul before birth? How many realms are there? Are fairies real? Do ghosts and spirits exist? Why are some people lucky and others unlucky, why is there suffering? Why are we here? Are there more things in the innocent-seeming world than we can see? These are some of the questions that the state of childhood asks, and which perplex us all our days.

Childhood is an enigma, a labyrinth, an existential question, a conundrum. It is the home of all the great questions about life and death, reality and dream, meaning and purpose, freedom and society, the spiritual and the secular, nature and culture, education and self-discovery.

3

Childhood is the Nile of life, the Eden, the Atlantis: the living emblem of mysterious places, vanished origins, lost beginnings, all that haunts because never to be found again. It is the cradle of future flowering, the celebrated place of innocence, of first loves, first evils, first falls, first sufferings, of first floods, and of the first civilisations within each human spirit. It is the Nile whose source leads to the illimitable.

4

Out of childhood rises the sphinx that is the adult. The sphinx who cannot pose its own riddle, much less answer it.

And yet from this Nile, from childhood, what personality is already present! Where did that distinct self come from? In what place intangible had that mind been gestating? In what universities of the invisible had this personality been preparing?

Its perspectives on the world surprise. The best observations of children ought to have a place in the academies of the world. It is not just the innocence of childhood that should command our attention. It is also its unseeing, or rather its pure seeing, uncontaminated by structures of habit. That way children sometimes have of perceiving things asequentially, tangentially. As though through the corridors of their minds clear winds of intuitions flow, hinting at the essential unreality of time and space.

How like a mature unlearning childhood is. Small wonder the sages throughout time use the state of childhood to speak of the highest things, the highest peaks of our cultural and spiritual attainment.

WRITERS AND NATIONS

1

There is no mystery about the decline of nations. It begins with the decline of its writers. Its first symptom is the nation's failure to celebrate its writers. Why is this so? Because writers represent the unconscious vigour and fighting spirit of a land.

2

Writers are the very sign of the psychic health of a people. They are the barometer of the vitality of the spirit of a nation. They are the beacon on the promontory signalling that here dwells a people strong enough to face its truths, brave enough to confront its demons, confident enough to diagnose the necessary drastic healing required for its malaise. They symbolise a people creative enough to dream new possibilities that will expand the psychic and moral resources of the land, and free enough to launch into great new adventures of the spirit. In this way true writers herald discovery, productivity, fertility, and resistance to spiritual despair. They embody that sublime sense of fearlessness in the challenging enterprise of civilisation.

3

When a nation celebrates its true writers, it celebrates itself. When a nation does not celebrate its writers it does not have much to celebrate. It does not have much to trumpet about itself to the world. It has no feats of the mind and spirit that it wishes to hold up to itself and to the world as visible signs of its shining accomplishments. Such a nation declares itself barren, dull, and spiritually bankrupt. It declares that it has lost the capacity to achieve things that rouse the sleeping powers of its citizens and capture the wandering imagination of the world. A nation that does not honour its truest, bravest, most creative, most enduring writers is a nation that has fallen out of love with itself.

4

Contemplate the literary frescoes of the ages. The Greeks were never more possessed of vitality and genius than when they had among them the living spectacle of their great tragedians; or when they bore in the casket of their hearts the magic force of Homer's words, as Alexander did while creating the new ages.

Look upon the era of Pericles, of Sophocles, Euripides, Thucydides, of Herodotus. Extend the vision to Virgilian Rome, when poets sang the ascending sunlight of the nation's soul into immortality. Think even of the writers like cracked oracles who cried out of the oncoming doom in imperishable words – that too was vitality.

Behold the vigour of the Elizabethans, of Shakespeare and Marlowe, and the sprawling intensity of their literature welling up like springs from rich underground streams. It was a golden age given space in its time. The wonder of the land that we all gaze back on in astonishment.

In Germany during the age of Goethe, the writers were the central force of the far-sighted spirit of the nation. The constellation of its poets, novelists, and playwrights created, in two generations, an extraordinary burst of luminous potential.

France too is a nation so alive to the practical and magical powers of the writer that its boulevards and roads celebrate their names as a public talisman. Thus it keeps active the very spirit of its great writers and their enduring works in the roads that its citizens walk along. This power, this value, is thus perpetually alchemising the consciousness of the people.

And so Rue Victor Hugo or Boulevard Voltaire are not just reminders of these great personalities who once wrote and shook the world; they make what is best in them present. The force that they have incarnated in the imagination is subtly impacted into the people's psyche, as they walk or drive down these roads.

Such a nation is never far from the spirit of creativity. It lives always in creativity's force field. Such a nation, even at its low points, always retains the power to charm. It also always contains the inclination to rise again to its former glory.

To celebrate, or to dwindle into dullness, seems to me the law at work here.

5

A nation's failure to honour its significant writers is a sign of imaginative impotence. Not to celebrate such greatness as it has annoys the gods for signal disregard of the gift of the spirit. To fail to appreciate the master-dreamers of our times is a sign that we cannot see what is good for us, or what is good in us.

It means that we do not recognise our own harvest, our own wonderful flowers, fruits, and trees. It means that we are not alive to our own good fortune, which we may as well not have. It is like living in poverty when gold and diamonds lie unrecognised among the weeds in our garden.

6

I have seen this principle at work on many continents. In Africa, during the first spring of freedom, its truth-loving writers sang, but not every nation listened, and decline and civil wars followed. Hopefully they will listen now.

Nations that imprison, torture, assassinate, or drive their writers into exile fall into the deadlands of their own darkness. No one loves such nations. Such nations do not love themselves.

7

Celebrate, or be dull. Appreciate, or be impoverished. Enhance, or give up the adventure of civilisation. Do not kill the romance of life. Most people want to live in brightened times. Most want to live in an air of enchantment, of creative challenge, of rich possibilities. Every child that becomes an adult wants to live in a world that breathes courage, imagination, and beautiful dreams. We all want the magic of that mythic sword that can conquer the darkness. There is no greater gift a people can be given than that they live a life touched with fable.

We ought to step out of our old, hard casing. We think we are one kind of people, when in fact we are always creating ourselves. We are not fixed. We are constantly becoming, constantly coming into being. Writers hold out the mirror to the bright visions of what we can be.

8

Honour that which should be honoured, or the spirit of the nation will quietly perish; and the nation will be the last to know this, for it will have forgotten how to dream.

SEEING AND BEING

Aphorisms

1

To see something one must first be something. One must become oneself.

2

To see what is going on in the art of the great writers or painters one must first of all be established in the art of oneself.

3

If one has not yet become oneself one cannot see the true self in others.

4

To see, one must first be.

5

All seeing depends first of all on being.

6

All the looking into the works of masters that we do before we have become ourselves is not true seeing, or it is missed seeing.

7

To see the true art or the truth in a work requires a solid foundation in oneself.

8

There must be a fully formed self for a fully formed seeing.

9

Otherwise like light passing through a transparent object the work of art passes straight through an unformed mind and heart.

10

It takes a work of art to see a work of art.

PLATO'S DREAM

The universities of the future will do one thing we do not do today. They will teach the art of self-discovery. There is nothing more fundamental in education.

We turn out students from our universities who know how to give answers, but not how to ask the essential questions. They leave universities with skills for the workplace, but with little knowledge of the best way to live, or what living is for.

They are not taught how to see. They are not taught how to listen. They are not taught how to connect with the wisdom in the world. They are not taught the art of obedience conjoined with intelligence, and how it precedes self-mastery.

They are not taught the art of reading. True reading is not just passing our eyes over words on a page, or even understanding what is being read. True reading is a creative act. It means seeing first; and then a subsequent act of the imagination. Higher reading ought to be a subject in the universities of the future. As we read, so we are.

On the whole, people do not actually read what is in front of them. They read what is only already inside them. I suspect this is true of listening; and that it is happening now, even as I speak to you, or as you read this page.

All our creativity, our innovations, our discoveries come from being able first to see what is there, and not there; to hear what is said, and not said. Above all to think clearly; to be nourished by silence. And beyond that – the art of intuition.

The universities of the future will have to engage the sublime value of intuition in our lives and work. How to make those intuitive leaps that can transform humanity, how to make this mysterious faculty available to all – this will be the true turning point in the future history of civilisation.

Discipline, hard work, rationality, calculation can get us only so far, and have become the norm. With these alone we produce efficient but mediocre citizens. But the art of intuition, the mysterious spark that separates the truly great artists and scientists and philosophers from the ordinary, this will one day have to be studied and developed in every human being for the highest benefits of the human race.

We need to teach students the inevitable necessity of self-discovery. Higher consciousness studies ought to be a fundamental part of education. All students ought to be philosophers. All students ought to be aware that they are the true spark for the transformation of the world. All students ought to be practical dreamers.

Universities ought not only to turn out students for the various spheres of business, science, the arts, and the general running of the society. They also need to awaken students into becoming people who enrich the life of the planet.

We are more than the jobs that we do. We are the co-makers of this world we live in. The moral force of citizens is too little used in the greater transformation of our world. We take the living potential that are young minds and turn them, reduce them, only into job-fillers and economy providers. We have regressed from Plato's dream – the wonderful project of his academy.

Every student is a light, a creative spark, waiting to be of use in dispelling the darkness. The terms in which I speak might seem alien, but will become inevitable.

Every day the crisis of purpose grows larger in the lives of people; and prosperity or poverty does not diminish the paralysis it will bring if not addressed. A lack of understanding why it exists, or of its larger purpose in the scheme of things, is how society quietly perishes.

The universe grows more mysterious around us even as we find out more about it. The true reason is this: we are more than we suspect, but we are taught to see less in ourselves, to ask no questions about our true inner nature. And so the great mystery within peers into the greater mystery without. A mystery stares into a mystery: this is a hopeless position.

We ought now to conjoin faith in evidence with a need

for self-discovery. Knowledge of self ought to be the great project of our lives. Knowing ourselves we will know others. Only by knowing ourselves can we begin to undo the madness we unleash on the world in our wars, our destruction of the environment, our divisions, our desire to dominate others, the poverty we create and exploit. Only through self-knowledge can we reverse the damage we do with all the worldly knowledge we have, which has been only a higher ignorance.

The true purpose of the university ought to be to unleash the sublime possibilities of the human spirit. Education is still in its infancy. The true education looms over the horizon, where our disasters are being born. There we will learn to avert what evils we ourselves have created. Then we will start again the great project of humanity, with humility and a new light.

ON CHILDHOOD (2)

1

Childhood ought to terrify us with gentle wonder. It ought to make us feel curiously humble. It has in it something akin to genius: there is simply no accounting for its everlasting appeal, its unfathomability.

I am speaking here of an aspect of childhood that lingers in the depths of the mind, like an imperishable melody. I am not speaking here of the other aspects of spoilt or conditioned or wretched childhoods that can be seen in nasty little boys or horrid little girls. I speak of the childhood seen out of the corner of the eye. I speak of the conjunction of its uncoordination and its magic, its serenity and its confusions. I speak of its multiple perspective. Its freedom, its lack of freedom.

2

That is why childhood also has something sad about it. For childhood is the place where tyranny rules absolutely, and of necessity. The child is moulded. That is the beginning of its fall, the loss of its Eden. To the child the world is named, explained, mis-explained, seamed with errors, made smaller, made plainer, made too complicated, narrowed, filled with suspicion, dogma, superstition and envy. Wonder is driven out from the world. Mystery is chased away from the fabric of reality. The tendency to ask questions is turned into a tendency to assume. The inclination to trust is warped into an inclination to fear. Flexibility is misrepresented as weakness. Sensitivity is distorted into timidity. The child is shaped; or should one say misshaped. Its open nature is closed off; its river canalised; its mind trapped; its spirit caged; its playfulness made forced; its joys made suspect; its laughter imprisoned.

3

The child should be shaped open, should be taught to value all peoples, to respect all races and creeds. But the child is taught to be suspicious of difference. A flower is thus changed into a thorn, a river into a brook, a garden into a wasteland.

The child is enveloped in the forms of a particular culture, when it could also be opened out to be at home in the world, with all its diversity. For when the child is born, it is born not into the ghetto, the palace, the villa but into the world, the open world. The child is born into the world of men and women, history and dreams, the limited and the limitless, the backyard and the sky. The child is born into an inheritance of all books, all thoughts, all the music and art and science that have been created in the perpetual pilgrimage of humanity along the dusty roads of time.

4

Childhood is the only time when the mind is so free, when fairies are as real as fires, when fables are true and reality is constantly invented. The world is a dream. And then the snake creeps in. Slowly corruption creeps in too, and the dream dies.

Hemingway writes somewhere of rich men and women in their yachts who weep at night because they can't sleep as purely as they did when they were children. More controversially, Blake writes that education is a sin. 'Improvement makes strait roads; but the crooked roads without improvement are roads of genius.'

5

Some people loathe their childhood because they were betrayed by it. I know of childhoods so severe, brutalised, and poverty-stricken that it's a wonder the children didn't become mass murderers. They turned out relatively sane. This is a continuing marvel. Even in the hardest of people there lurks something of childhood's elusive twilight. It may be distorted, but it is there. It comes out in what these hard people love, what they are sentimental about, or even, paradoxically, in what they hate.

THE ROMANCE OF DIFFICULT TIMES

1

All things in life are governed by the law of cycles.

2

There can be no rise without a fall, no fall without a rise.

3

There can be no prosperity without adversity that has been wisely transformed.

4

A glance at the history of civilisations reveals their humble and difficult beginnings. Think of the fall of Troy and what Virgil created out of that disaster: the wanderings and adversity of the people who became the future Roman Empire.

5

The *Aeneid* reminds us that great civilisations can be built on great failures. It also reminds us that adversity is not the end of a story but, where there is courage and vision, the beginning of a new one, a greater one than before.

6

Difficult times do one of two things to us: they either break us or they force us to go back to the primal ground of our being.

7

Adversity wakes us up. It reminds us not of who we think we are in our vanity, but who we really are in our simplicity.

8

Success makes us fly with unreal wings and more often than not, like Icarus, takes us too close to the sun.

9

But adversity reminds us that the earth is that on which we stand. We feel our feet on this earth. We learn to walk again with our feet on good solid ground.

10

There are few blessings more solid than being made to take the measure of ourselves.

11

Too often we go through life with vague dreams, wild goals or no goals at all.

12

When we are successful we believe in the rightness of our whims and thought. We believe the most inflated things about ourselves. We mythologise our abilities. We think of ourselves, secretly, as gods. This can only last so long either in the life of nations or individuals. And this is disastrous for true growth. It prepares a fall sooner or later.

13

Adversity tells us the truth of how things stand. It never deceives, never inflates, never lies.

14

Success can send us flying off in wrong directions for a long time. One need think only of the bloated complacency of the Persian Empire before its catastrophic encounter with the lean disciplined force of Alexander the Great.

15

The highest point of a great civilisation is not necessarily its golden age: that is merely the fructification. The highest point is actually in its earlier stages, after a people have worked their way out of a long adversity, having disciplined themselves, and faced their truths, and conceived worthwhile and magnificent goals, and moved steadily towards them with faith and a rapture of overcoming.

Alexander after the conquest of Darius; England in the Elizabethan age: this is where a people most becomes itself.

16

In the midst of adversity, face what needs to be faced.

17

'Sometimes the way up is the way down,' Heraclitus said.

18

For there to be a new prosperity we must first have a new adversity.

19

It is in difficult times that the great times ahead are dreamt and built, brick by brick, with maturity and the hope that comes from wise action.

20

Difficult times, in retrospect, are more romantic than good times, if they are overcome. Myths and fables are made of them.

Photography and Immortality

To Sandy Nairne

Photography ought to be seen as a species of magic, but we have lost our innocence. And so we see it as an aspect of reality.

There is no art by which to reproduce the lineaments of the real. Each human face will always be unique in skin, flesh, and features. Any attempt at exact reproduction loses the contours, the three-dimensionality, and the living quality of the individual face. What photography achieves in portraiture is not a reproduction but a refiguration, a translation from one dimension to another.

Something strange happens in this process: the human face is alienated. It is a metamorphosis in reverse. The face is thus simplified. The curved quality of space is flattened. Light is reduced in source and effect.

Portraiture is the dialogue of light and the face, in the dimension of memory. That is why the portrait is not the person. It is an abstracted memory, enriched by time.

Three principles make portraiture unique: light, the subject, and time. Of these three, the most alchemical is time. Time is the magic mercury, the fifth element, the quintessence. It is the constantly transforming and preserving substance of portraiture.

Time acts with the shutter speed. It acts with the speed of light that travels to the subject, from the subject to the camera, and from the photograph to our eyes.

There is an internal time that is also at work from the first mental encounter with the image to its interactions in the vast realm of memory. A realm perpetually impinged on by desire, loss, and life's infinitely shaded experiences.

Time weaves a spell round the image – preserves it, changes it. Portraiture keeps the subject in its time and yet projects it into ours.

Portraiture is always time travel. It is a time travel that keeps all the secrets of its time concealed behind the subject. It freights over to us only the image, mute with all the passions of life.

Silent stories stare out from those eyes. They will no longer look upon the light or dark of our day. And yet they look at us as through a transparent medium, beyond even death. What is the true nature of that almost mystic medium?

There is a hint of immortality in all portraiture. The subjects live, in another dimension, alien to us. They live, but they are motionless. Time has gone from them, yet still they persist in time. They live in an enigma.

Does their image differ from the memory we have of them? Is memory truer?

Portraiture suggests a parallel memory in the universe, in which all things persist. Photography touches us so mysteriously because we have an intuition that all things are remembered in some invisible place beyond dreams, where everything that was exists in a sort of universal, divine amber.

Many wonderful notions ought to flash past one's mind in the presence of these people upon whom time has wrought an enchantment.

Portraiture ought to remind us that we live between two enigmas, birth and death. Photography is the dream, the interval, which we take to be the real.

And yet secret tears flow behind these portraits. We too will be like them.

But we have lost our innocence. Otherwise these images ought to start in us a new philosophy of living, a new simplicity, and maybe even a new happiness.

HOSPITALITY

1

Hospitality begins in the soul.

2

Hospitality is more than a rational, deliberate act. It is a way of being.

3

Hospitality ought to be built into a people's way of living.

4

A people can only live the art of hospitality if they transform what they are.

5

Hospitality is not a habit. It is a genius of self that recognises the genius of other selves.

6

Hospitality takes us back to the root of humanity, the source of rivers.

7

Hospitality is not tolerance or charity, nor is it weakness. Hospitality can only come from the true strength of knowing what one is, and the tranquillity of allowing other people the strength of what they are.

8

Hospitality is a secret affirmation of the oneness of humanity, a sort of secular kinship. Hospitality is something we should be able to extend not just to our friends, but even to our enemies.

9

The idea of hospitality is challenged most when we are dealing with the unknown. It means that we have faith first even before we have evidence.

10

The ideal of hospitality does not die even when it has been betrayed, but is only made wiser.

11

Hospitality requires courage and wisdom.

12

According to Lao Tsu the truest hospitality is when the host is like a guest, and the guest like a host.

13

The limits of hospitality were revealed most in colonialism. We all know what happened to the hospitality of the Incas towards the Spaniards, and the Africans towards the Europeans. The Incas were slaughtered, robbed, and became victims of genocide. And the Africans still have not recovered from that early foolish kind of hospitality where the host is ignorant about the world and the true intentions of the visitors.

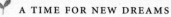

14

Hospitality has to be both wise and sane.

15

Philosophically there is no such thing as hospitality because we are all guests on this planet, we are all guests in life.

16

Didn't Auden say about Yeats when he died, 'Earth receive an honoured guest'?

17

In fact it is quite possible that we are guests in the universe and guests in the condition of mortal consciousness.

18

Hospitality is therefore temporary, finite, and subject to the continual changes of the human condition.

19

Today I am a guest, tomorrow I am a host.

20

There is also intellectual hospitality, the hospitality to ideas, to dreams, to ways of seeing, to perception, to cultures. We will call this invisible hospitality. This is the most important hospitality of all and it includes all other hospitalities.

21

Beyond that we are talking about the hospitality of the infinite, which should be pursued in silence and through initiation, following a secret path towards the eternal.

O, YE WHO INVEST IN
FUTURES

1

It is easy to dismiss Africa. It is easy to patronise Africa. It is easy to profess to like Africa. It is easy to exploit Africa. And it is easy to insult Africa.

But it is difficult to see Africa truly. It is difficult to see its variety, its complexity, its simplicity, its individuals. It is difficult to see its ideas, its contributions, its literature. It is difficult to hear its laughter, understand its cruelties, witness its spirituality, withstand its suffering, and grasp its ancient philosophies.

Africa is difficult to see because it takes heart to see her. It takes simplicity of spirit to see her without confusion. And it takes a developed human being to see her without prejudice.

2

Africa is a challenge to the humanity and sleeping wisdom of the world. It is an eyeball-challenging enigma. Africa reveals what most hides in people. It reveals their courage or cowardice, their complacency or their conscience, their smallness or their generosity. Faced with Africa, nothing of what you truly are can hide. Africa brings to light the true person beneath their politeness, their diplomacy, or their apparent good intentions.

Africa is the challenge of the human race in the twenty-first century because, through her, humanity can begin to feel at peace with itself. Africa is our conscience. There can be no true progress for humanity till the sufferings of our brother and sister continents are overcome, till people everywhere live reasonably good lives, free from vile diseases, undernourishment, illiteracy and tyranny.

3

There is another sense in which Africa – for those who do not know her – is difficult to see. To see Africa one must first see oneself.

The laziness of the eyes has to go. It won't do any more to let our hearts and minds be affected by the colour of someone's skin. This problem, amazingly, is still here. It is one of the silent tragedies of our times. It prevents people making true friends. It prevents them reading the literature of others. It hinders the flow of ideas and the mutual enrichment of our lives. More often than not culture is colour-biased. We are still primitives in the art of being human.

4

This is what gives literature its sublime importance. Literature makes it possible to encounter others in the mind first. Literature is the encounter of possibilities, the encounter of the work and the heart. It is the true ambassador of the unity of humankind.

5

When I visit the houses of acquaintances a cursory glance at their bookshelves reveals everything I need to know, regardless of what they profess.

It is easy enough to have bookshelves weighed down with formidable rows of Shakespeare, Dickens, Jane Austen, Thomas Hardy, or Henry James, and all else that has acquired the patina of the classical. It is easy enough to have a fashionable collection of writers we deem to display a progressive tendency, alongside the popular books of the day.

But to have novels by Ukrainians, Iranians, Indians, Egyptians, poems by an unknown Samoan, a Dutch collection of stories, works by Kenyan, Nigerian, Jamaican novelists, plays from Portugal, Japanese elegies, all mixed in with books that reveal a healthy interest in what the human spirit is dreaming; now that is something special. For here would be a person that Goethe would have called a citizen of the world. Here would be a person one would want to have as a friend, a person keen on humanity, fascinated by its varied genius.

6

That's what this is about: celebrating the genius of human diversity. The idea is to enrich the world by its greater contact with Africa, and to enrich Africa by its greater contact with the world. The dream is to create a bridge of the imagination. The hope is to share in the fun and the marvel of the creative spirit.

7

It is not enough just to pass one's eyes over the words, to read literature passively. That would be like what Mozart said about his mother-in-law: 'She would see the opera, but not hear it.' We should read this literature with an open mind, an intelligent heart.

True literature tears up the script of what we think humanity to be. It transcends the limitations we impose on the possibilities of being human. It dissolves preconceptions. True literature makes us deal with something partly new and partly known. That is why we can't ask new literature to be like the old, to give us the same pleasures as those that have gone before. That wouldn't be living literature, which surprises and redefines. That would be mere repetition.

Literature mirrors, reveals, liberates.

8

Literature from Africa has long been in the margins. One of the benefits of this is that it has much to do. It has so many new moods, possibilities, philosophies to bring into being. This literature will bring many unsuspected gifts and wonderful surprises to the world in the fullness of time.

9

O, ye who invest in Futures, pay heed to Africa. Today she is wounded and is somewhat downcast. But tomorrow she will flower and bear fruit, as the Nile once flowered into the Pyramids, or like the savannahs after the rains.

10

Africa has a weird resilience. Her future bristles with possibilities. When she heals, Africa will amaze.

Dramatic Moments in the Encounter between Picasso and African Art

An Essay in Ricochet

Encounter

When he saw the masks he was shattered by the original flash of lightning, with its zigzag out of nothing. A howl and a laughter as mysterious as the map of Africa clouded his mind.

In that moment all of ancient Spain died and was resurrected in a new form. The golden proportion perished and was reborn in an obscure dance in the dark. The tentative perfection of Raphael, the exquisite mystery of Da Vinci, the electrified gap between the outstretched finger of an indolent Adam and the life-giving power of the original father, all were destroyed and remade in a miraculous exchange of energy.

In that moment the mass of the past was multiplied by a consciousness illumined by the speed of light squared. And in less than a moment he beheld an image in the dark that confronted two thousand years of beauty.

In that flash of a moment a wild new symmetry was born. A savage new aesthetic came into being. A new century and a new world dawned.

The ancient masks confounded, at a stroke, the reasoning that had enslaved their makers and blurred the God that had destroyed the gods. And a new religion without a name would haunt the eyes of the Western dreamers as a revenge for the enlightenment that went wrong. An enlightenment that, as well as liberating, also created a new slavery, a new darkness.

And so for the first time in centuries the different sides of the spirit of man collided. In that fusion the unstable reign of beauty came to an end. It was no longer sustainable in a world where men had killed God in their hearts. An implosion of energy took the form of a possession. A howl and a jubilation of destruction, a cry of power from the future throat of the blinded minotaur, seized the young man in a grip so pure that for a moment he was blinded by the masks.

He saw the world with their eyes. He understood the meaning of his life and his vocation. He grasped the true mystery and necessity of art. He became its willing and fortunate slave. He became the high priest at the shrine of an unknown god. And he was blessed with the ambiguous power he so craved over the minds of men.

He had been touched into life by the ancient myth of the superman and by the brilliant angel of the beautiful darkness. A darkness that was, in truth, a new light.

All this took less than a moment.

The moment when his eyes gazed, for the first time, at the masks.

Possession

They had been whispering among themselves, the masks and sculptings. The spirits had been in great dialogue with one another. They had been debating how best to get their weird wisdom to enter into the broad stream of humanity. They debated how to make their mysteries alive in the new times. How to be valuable among people who were at a crossroads, and who had come to the end of a way of seeing.

The masks ceased their whispering when a young Spaniard came amongst them in the museum where they dwelled. The Spaniard had fierce eyes and his soul was hungry for newness and for a sorcerer's power. This was a young man crowded with questions.

The spirits ceased their speech when they beheld the young Spanish painter who had already made a pact with an unknown divine force that he would give up art if someone he loved, who was ill, was spared from death. But the divine force, in infinite wisdom beyond cruelty, had seized the life of the loved one, and left the young painter with an immortal contract. He must create art, or die. He must create great art or suffer eternal perdition of the soul for not fulfilling his pact with the eternal powers.

The spirits beheld this troubled and deeply hungry young artist and they knew they had found what they were seeking. The foundations of art were deep in him. His psychic frame was tough. And yet he had great spaces in him, gaps craving a new way. The spirits knew what they must do. They would possess this young artist's soul. They would infect his spirit with new vision. They would use him to make their secret ways and higher energies known to the world, in the new age. Among strangers who had almost lost the sense of wonder, they would be the annunciation of an oblique golden age.

And so, in silence, and as one, the spirits leapt into the young artist's eyes, into his blood, and nestled in his soul. They took over his art, and seized the power of his hand. Being more powerful than his young will, they made him do what they wanted him to do, but through the filter, the mediation of his rich artistic sensibility.

From that moment, he fell into a dream, an obscure possession. He was never his old self again, as an artist, or a man. And to survive henceforth, he condemned himself to the necessity of perpetual transformation, trying to escape that which had already changed him, and would go on changing him for as long as he lived.

Thus two destinies were fulfilled. The destiny of the masks to alter the art of the world. And the destiny of an artist to fulfil his pact with the ambiguous powers of the universe ...

Afterwards, when the artist woke from the dream, from the possession, he found all these works he had created. No one understood them for many years. They were enigmas.

He could never satisfactorily explain how they had come to be. For the magic of that moment never happened again. All the words of denial and affirmation he used to explain the mystery of his artistic discoveries only made the mystery more strange ...

Meanwhile, the spirits and the masks had moved on. They took their secrets with them into the depths of their unfathomable African silence. There the truth of things resonates in eternal renewal among the gods.

Obsession

I've got to do something amazing or die. I've got to seize my power or be destroyed. I've got to stage a coup against life, against the past, against beauty, against poverty, against love, against death, against failure, against the ancients, against the ancestors, against the future, or I'll perish.

I've got to find a new power. I've got to find a new source. I've got to find, I've got to find, I've got to find, or I'll never live. I've got to find freedom. I've got to breathe a new air. I've got to find a new world. I've got to find a new consciousness. I've got to find a new continent. I've got to find new eyes. I've got to see with new eyes.

I've got to find a new beauty, a new religion, a new dawn, a new faith, a new family, a new time, a new energy, a new life, a new body, a new sex, a new laughter, a new mystery.

I've got to find a new creation. I've got to find a new beginning. I've got to find a new art, a new now, a new present without a past and without a future, an eternal present always present.

I've got to find a new fame. I've got to find what no one

has found and what no one will find again. I've got to find the unfindable, or I am finished, or I am unbegun, I may as well die, but I can't die, I won't die. I'll wrestle with eternity if I have to. I'll wrestle with the angels of light and darkness if I must. I'll exchange my blood for a new blood made of the ink and oils of a new art. I'll do a deal with the dark one himself and I'll wriggle out of his claws if I have to. But I've got to find, for I feel death on my back, the death of all that's gone before that will not last the new harsh light that we have made to chase away the mysteries.

I've got to do something to split time apart. I've got to do something to split life into its splinters of pure beauty, the beauty of a new source of energy for the mind's eternal delight.

I've got to do something astonishing, for I am being destroyed by the ancient fathers. I'm being destroyed by two thousand years of beauty and tradition and unfreedom. I'm being destroyed by reason. I'm being destroyed by faith. I'm being destroyed by materialism, and by science. I'm being destroyed by the Church and its dogmas and its incomplete truths about the true mystery and meaning of it all. I'm being destroyed by art, by literature, by the academies, by the Renaissance.

I'm being destroyed by too much thought, too many notions, too many oracles, too many dictates, too many laws, too many dos and don'ts. I'm being destroyed by too many empires and wars, and tyrannies of the mind, too many idols.

I'm not yet born and the burden of too much false knowledge, from Mount Olympus to Mount Everest, is on my back. I'm full of too many myths and all the myths of Greece and Rome and Europe and home are killing and choking me with their too-muchness. And I long to destroy them all or resolve or dissolve them all into a pure tincture or dew.

I'm being destroyed by too many books, too many ideas, too many prophecies, too many philosophies, too many discoveries, too many geniuses, too many broken titans and towering charlatans.

I'm being destroyed by too much knowledge that is too much ignorance. All the discoveries have been made, they say, and there is nothing new under the sun, but I must find something new in the darkness of the sun. For too much light hides and creates its own darkness, its own blindness. And there is much we are not seeing with our eyes wide open because we are using our eyes and seeing not that which we see but that which we have seen before. And so I have to destroy the old eyes. I have to destroy the old light that prevents us truly seeing. I have to invent or find a new darkness in which we can truly see.

I have got to do something amazing, for everything that gave birth to me in the mind and body and heart is killing me in my birth. I've got to find a new fire to burn away my birth, and burn up all the idols of the past, all the gods of art, all the idols of culture, burn them all up as I was burned into life, as they burned the masks of the Africans in the great bonfire of Empire. So too I must burn all that imprisons me as a child of the earth. And then I must do what that god of fire did, give a new light, a new fire to myself in my new birth of power, or I'll die in this darkness that is the anarchy of our times.

I sense mighty changes coming, and grim horrors, and nightmares from which we will not awaken for a hundred years. I sense monsters in time that will be seen as saviours. I sense evils clothed in light. I sense terrors in the obscure seeds of time, storms without mercy, and worse evils in man undreamt of before, sleeping in the mass of the overcrowding ruins of our past which we mistake for ancient glories.

The new century sleeps and who knows what vile dreams it will unleash when it is goaded awake by guns and the sleep of reason? I sense them all and they are killing me before I am born, and I must find the power to give them form, to seize their power, and exorcise them before they get us. For I must be free and must do something to protect this dream which is me.

I am ready to die to be born. I am ready to receive a new form, a new sacrament, a new passion. I will serve at the rigorous altar of truth if I can be free of this tyrannical burden of orthodox beauty that conceals unsuspected evils, into which I was born.

I will be the willing pilgrim of a new way of finding if I can destroy this dying weight of tradition and rebuild it again in six days.

I must do something transcendent, for I will not die.

I will defy death with my secret eyes.

Dialogue of the Masks

In a language which human beings cannot hear, the masks spoke to one another in their angular silence.

Spirit 1: They do not see us, these living ones that do not know how to live.

Spirit 2: They do not see much.

Spirit 1: Even with their eyes wide open.

Spirit 2: Especially with their eyes wide open.

Spirit 1: They can open their eyes as wide as the sky and still they will not see much.

Spirit 2: They can have their eyes as bright as fire and still they will not see much.

Spirit 1: Our ancestors were right. The more you look, the less you see.

Spirit 2: The more you see, the less you look.

Spirit 1: If you look you will not see.

Spirit 2: If you see you will not need to look.

Spirit 1: The more you look the more you look.

Spirit 2: The more you see the more you see.

Spirit 1: But these living ones, they do not see us and they do not see themselves.

Spirit 2: Words prevent them from seeing.

Spirit 1: They talk too much.

Spirit 2: And too soon.

Spirit 1: What they see is not there.

Spirit 2: What is there they do not see.

Spirit 1: They think too much.

Spirit 2: I can hear them when they think.

Spirit 1: Their thinking is loud.

Spirit 2: They think that they think.

Spirit 1: They think that thinking is thinking in words.

Spirit 2: Their thinking is without much thought.

Spirit 1: They think themselves into not seeing.

Spirit 2: They think themselves into not feeling.

Spirit 1: They think themselves into not being.

Spirit 2: They think themselves into not living.

Spirit 1: They ought to be taught how not to think.

Spirit 2: The art of non-thinking.

Spirit 1: The art of being.

Spirit 2: Then they will begin the great thinking.

Spirit 1: But will they listen?

Spirit 2: No.

Spirit 1: Will they learn?

Spirit 2: No.

Spirit 1: What is to be done?

Spirit 2: Nothing. Only to confound them with our silence.

Spirit 1: Our stillness.
Spirit 2: Our stillness in which there is immortal motion.
Spirit 1: Our stillness in which the words of the gods work.
Spirit 2: Our stillness full of magic.
Spirit 1: Our silence full of music.
Spirit 2: Our silence full of immortal harmonies.
Spirit 1: Our stillness full of immortal mysteries.
Spirit 2: We will confound them.
Spirit 1: And live.

Sublimation

I want to be a new beginning and an end. Creation will return to its source again, in a zigzag flash of reverse lightning.

After me there will be no habits of seeing, no standards of doing set in immortal stone. I want to destroy the old artistic commandments. New worlds would be created from a new ground.

After me, nothing. And in that nothing something is born from brave new souls, something like paradise, drifting in from the horizon.

On Childhood (3)

1

Childhood: being under the care of those who are generally ill qualified to be parents. People ought to learn to be parents before they become parents. It should be more than just a biological inevitability.

2

Childhood: focus of love – real love and confused love.

3

Childhood: the meeting place of an endless chain of failures and successes, hopes and fears, marvels and disasters, disorders and joys, and the hidden narrative of ancestors. Childhood is the inheritor of concentrated fictions invisible.

Every child is an entire literature. All tragedies, comedies, and epics are already resident in its birth.

4

Childhood: a lottery, Chardin's game of cards, the luck of the draw, an unsuspected gamble, an obscure mathematics of destiny or karma; an unspecified punishment or an unnamed blessing – for deserving the parents you have, the family you're stuck with, or the life you were born into.

5

Childhood: a time also of innocent cruelties, tearing off the wings of butterflies, cutting up worms, ganging up on the weakest, the newcomer, or the strange one. Who hasn't noticed the peculiar intolerance of childhood; the unqualified ego of the state; or the games, the toy guns, the locking up of the smallest in a shed and then forgetting . . .

6

Childhood: the place of all society's experiments, its disastrous ideas of conscious engineering.

7

Childhood: in legend reared by wolves, the child becomes wolf-like. Reared by strangers, the child has something of the stranger within them.

8

Childhood: the place where so many seeds and notions are planted in us, and watered with the loving hands of our parents, and become full-grown trees of appalling prejudices, deeply held secret resentments, fiercely guarded dragons of suspicions, hydra-headed monsters of superstitions. All of these lovingly or bitterly planted in us and absorbed by us with all the full reverence and unquestioning acceptance we give to our parents when our minds are young and theirs to mould.

It is a difficult thing indeed to free our minds of the errors of our parents. For it amounts to rewriting our childhood, tearing down its mysterious palaces, stripping our parents of the mythical place they have within us. It would mean conceding our parents a certain ordinariness, like any other parent of one's age group that one might think of as a bit of a fool and yet to their child is a god ...

Who can disarrange the fragile garden of childhood and not make themselves a little poorer for it?

9

In literature childhood is an invention, a creation, a state constructed. The literature of childhood is properly either historical fiction, or imaginative reconstruction.

Childhood is a fairy tale taking place in a chaos. Childhood is not aware of itself as childhood.

10

Notice how late the literature of childhood appeared in the ancient world. The literature of childhood seems to suggest that society has passed its phase of childhood, its era of unconscious consciousness, its period of myths and legends, of living fables, heroic deeds, difficulties, beginnings. This literature suggests a new phase of nostalgia, of loss. The literature of childhood signifies that for a nation or a people its golden age is over. They look back who have crossed the hill. When a society has lost its way, it looks back thus – to childhoods, to origins, to arcadias. This implies a prevalent chaos, and a longing for simplicity, away from confusion.

A literature of childhood is an implicit criticism of the present. It can often be a quiet, decisive political act. It can be a scream woven into a melody, a beautiful song thrown into the face of tyranny. It can be a transfigured form of guerrilla warfare against the psyche of repression, a howl from the wounded heart of innocence. Or it can be an act of exile from the intolerable present.

11

Nations are best when you can still see something of the openness of the child in the grown-ups: a wisdom that arcs towards mature simplicity, like ancient temples.

10½ INCLINATIONS*

1   There is a secret trail of books meant to inspire and enlighten you. Find that trail.

2   Read outside your nation, colour, class, gender.

3   Read the books your parents hate.

4   Read the books your parents love.

5   Have one or two authors that are important, that speak to you; and make their works your secret passion.

6   Read widely, for fun, for stimulation, for escape.

7   Don't read what everyone else is reading. Check them out later, cautiously.

8   Read what you're not supposed to read.

9   Read for your own liberation and mental freedom.

10   Books are like mirrors. Don't just read the words. Go into the mirror. That is where the real secrets are. Inside. Behind. That's where the gods dream, where our realities are born.

10½   Read the world. It is the most mysterious book of all.

---

* The Royal Society of Literature asked 10 writers to suggest the 10 books that children should read before leaving school. Instead of a list of books, I wrote this.

SELF-CENSORSHIP

1

Much has been said about public censorship, but not enough about self-censorship. We veil our thoughts from ourselves. We censor our true feelings about the outrages of our day. We accept a great deal of lies from the powers that be. We swallow whole what we are fed in the various media of information and misinformation.

We are easy to manipulate because we absorb without thinking. And when we do think, we think what we have thought before. We do not question enough. We do not apply sufficient rigour to the information we receive and the conclusions that can be drawn from it. We collude in the great follies and injustices of our age by censoring our minds.

They do things in our name, with our votes, using our silent consent. Then much later our children are horrified to learn that we were present and adult when unacceptable outrages against humanity were perpetrated under our very noses, and that we did nothing. And so we implicate a whole generation; and, in extreme cases, a whole nation.

It is only by being free in ourselves that we can extend the freedom of others. It is only by being free that we can guarantee clean hands for the next generation to fight the good fight of their era.

It is time we considered the bedrock of censorship – and this is the censorship that takes place within.

We stifle our most humane thoughts. We silence our impulses to translate our sense of injustice into action. We sense something is wrong but we choose to be silent. Sometimes we do this just to have a quiet life. Sometimes we are silent because it has always been some kind of national characteristic. Embarrassment, not wanting to be different, not wanting to be the only one voicing dissent are kinds of self-censorship.

Traditional modes of behaviour are internalised forms that become part of the matrix of self-censorship.

We are victims of censorship within when we do not let ourselves think the thoughts which our flesh recoils from, or let conscience speak that which the heart feels to be unacceptable, or when we give ourselves excellent reasons for not participating in this grand drama of our interconnected lives. Then we make it possible for governments to censor all those who speak out when they find our freedoms being crushed, visibly or invisibly.

2

There are many nations across the world where great works could be created, but they are not. Generations have come and gone and there have been no works of significant creativity amongst them. Didn't the people suffer, dream, love, or endure oppression? Didn't history, with its trap-doors, its earthquakes, its upheavals, happen to them? Was there no evil, no failure, no loss, no rage, no quests, no doubts, no yearning for something undefinable? Then why so little to show for all that perplexity of living and dying, of loving and weeping, of betrayals and forgiveness? Why nothing to show for all that fire? The reason may just be censorship within.

They dared not think that which they should think. They dared not differ. They dared not step outside the prevailing orthodoxies. There are, maybe, other reasons. That under fear of death, exile, torture, the murder of loved ones, the threat to their livelihood, their government drives into silence the conscience that could express itself through the oblique forms of the imagination. In short, the artists censor themselves. The forces that be kill creativity at the very place of conception, in the heart, before inspiration can hover over the mind like that dove of the holy spirit.

And then we say the people were without genius. They lived as if they didn't live. They gave us no sign that they were here. They added nothing to the ongoing battle for the higher civilisation of humanity. They bequeathed us nothing, not even hope. They might as well have sunk to the bottom of the sea, or vanished without a trace.

So it will be of us, if we are not mindful. We live in an age of monstrosities. We fiddle while the last days of the earth draw closer, thanks to our mindlessness. Wars rage under our eyes. Famines and plagues devour our neighbours across the seas. Next door someone is dying for want of care. Our children, with insufficient moral guidance, are burning up the tattered bible of tolerance, patience, and understanding. Anomie and indifference take on glamorous names.

How can we care about big things afar when big things nearby are not seen, even as they consume us? The true issue of our age is not terrorism or religion. The great issue of our age is freedom.

We need to de-censor our minds. Much has been said about the damage done to all when our freedom of expression is destroyed. Now it is time to speak of the more insidious censorship upon which rest the more sensational censorships.

O fellow members of the human race, de-censor your minds. The mind is the only true place of freedom. Let's protect that freedom within by constantly asking questions, by thinking clearly, by transcending our traditional and habitual modes of thought. That way we will better protect one another from having our world ruined by those who rule in our name, who sometimes have no idea of the catastrophic effects of what they are doing. Let's raise our voices when our consciences are choked. Only free people can make a free world.

One Planet, One People

An Address to Students

Be wiser than your fathers and mothers. Be bigger-hearted. I know your fathers and mothers, and they are good people, and I love them, but you will be bigger-hearted.

You are the real hope and possibility of the century. Do not accept any limitation on the definition of what is human, and what is possible to humanity. Do not box anyone in. Don't let yourself be boxed in either. Tear down all barriers of race, class, gender, religion, and sexual orientation. Believe in the fundamental equality of humanity.

Link hands with your brothers and sisters across the globe. Link hands with the poor and the disadvantaged and the rich. Don't look down at anyone and don't look up at anyone either. You are not better than the poor, nor inferior to the rich. The heritage of the earth is for all of us. Make this world one world, its riches and possibilities available to all.

Do not think for one moment that you are small, that you are powerless, that you have nothing to give, or that you are alone. I have not met a powerless person. You are only small and powerless if you think only of yourself, if you are selfish. The moment you think of humanity, of service to humanity, then you become powerful.

The heart is bigger than the earth. There are few things more noble in this life than serving humanity. If ever you suffer from crises of confidence, from doubt, from fear, from suicidal impulses, from loneliness, from existential despair, that is often because you are living only for yourself, your career, your dreams, your ego, your race, your family, clan or class. But the moment you think of humanity, all humanity, then your own problems become smaller, and then disappear.

We are here on earth to serve humanity, to take the human possibility forward, to create a better world. We are here to grow, to learn, to share our light, our gifts, our love.

There are people who are prepared to die for their limited racial and religious causes. They are a negative inspiration.

You should be prepared to be the most wonderful person you are capable of being, and for the best causes, which are the enrichment of humanity, the promotion of equal rights for all, the provision of education, food, and a good life for the poor and wretched of the earth. This is a greater way to live than even laying down your life for your brother, sister, or your country.

Use all the intelligence, passion, fun, joy, and the blessings of your life to help make the life of all humanity sweeter, and you will not have to worry unduly about the state of your soul or about the meaning of life. If you do this alone, especially in this part of your life when you are young and free, if you give what's good in you to raising higher the human story as best you can, then your life will be justified, and you will have transcended failure and success.

Open your hearts and minds to the beauties and possibilities of being human. Do not see people's colour first. Do not see people in their material conditions first. We don't know who or what any human being really is. Believe me, we are each one a great mystery. The person who dwells in great misery, in the gutter, alone, may well be an angel. The way you judge others – a person or a continent – judges you. And this judgement will bring you either the good or the evil you deserve.

So, go out into the world. Transcend all the bullshit that your education, your history, your culture, your class has passed on to you. Learn for yourselves. Find out for yourselves. Question everything. Question the certainties fed you by your mothers and fathers and the great authority figures of your land and your age. Be always a question mark. Seek to know for yourself, so that you may grasp the deeper truths of life with a strong mind. Give of your soul. Feel the life and the suffering and the joys of the world. Feel! Don't be afraid to feel, or to love, or to fail. So long as you are doing the little best you can to make this ruined world better, you are making good use of the miraculous reality that is your life.

For the rest, have fun. Laugh. Lighten up. Don't be too serious. Play. Be inspired. Be your true best self without being mean to others. And, by God, learn the wonderful art of happiness. We not only deserve to be happy. It is our divine right. How can we enjoy the happiness and growth of others, if we are not happy ourselves? It was Novalis who said: 'I am you' – in another form.

Let life inspire you, and teach you always how to be free, and to encourage freedom in others, if they so desire.

All of humanity is really one person. What happens to others, affects us. There's no way out, but up.

Let's all rise to the beautiful challenges of our age, and rise to our true mysterious luminosity.

LONDON, OUR FUTURE CITY

An Orientation

For Chris Smith

A city is only as great as the dreams that can be realised there. The more beautiful the dreams, the greater the city.

After all, cities are made by men and women; but the city that allows the highest aspirations and possibilities of its people, its artists, its visionaries, its architects, its administrators to flourish and shine becomes the magic city of the world. Such a city everyone wants to make a pilgrimage to, and hopes to dwell in for a time, as one of the great adventures in living. James Baldwin said that what is valued by a people is what is found amongst them. London's future can be no better therefore than what we value, the true quality of our dream.

Dostoevsky said famously that St Petersburg is the most intentional city in the world. He meant, I imagine, that it was shaped deliberately, made consciously. There are two sides to this. An intentional city, shaped by genius, becomes a dream of genius. But geniuses rarely get to shape cities. Too many factors prevent this, not least the factor of pragmatism. On the other hand, cities ought to have in them something organic, something intrinsic. They ought to grow from their own dream, their character, their ever-unfolding identity. They ought to be like a work of art made by many master artists, animated by the same magical vision.

I have used the word 'dream' a lot in this meditation. And that is because a great city is a dream, a great dream. We do practical things there like work, play, and live; but the most important thing we do in a city is different from what we do in nature. And that is we create future possibilities from an ever-revealing, ever-concealing present. This can only be done where there is space, the space in which a higher life can flourish. This space is not just the space of parks, cathedrals, or between buildings. I speak of another kind of space. First let me play a little on this theme.

On the whole cities tend to be too built-up. City planners seldom see a space that they are not tempted to fill. We treat space as an element of functionality. We always think that space should be doing something, or that we should always do something in a space. For that reason we tend, either in thought or in reality, to bulk up all our spaces.

If a space is not being used, isn't being filled up, we think of it as useless, or as dead space. We also have this attitude to time, which is another form of space. And so we create a world of diminishing space.

But if there is one great potential of humanity it is precisely in the freedom, the potentiality, of spaces. The most important space of all is the space to dream, the space to be free, the space to conceive and unfold the magical project of humanity.

Such a space cannot be a real space, like a park, a green belt, or a skyline, though I believe passionately that these spaces should be cultivated. The one I hint at has its home primarily in the dreams of a city, in the minds and hearts of its people. It is a mental space, or rather a space rich in potential for ideas and deeds of genius that can reside in and come from the mind.

What am I really saying? As within, so without; as without, so within, goes the ancient adage. What we see in our city is what we have planted there from our hearts or from our heartlessness, from our vision or lack of it. Everything outside has come from inside. And many things inside us have come from outside us. We either create a city that dehumanises us, or one that transforms us by its aspirations, its symbols, its visible wisdom.

I dream of a new kind of city. Not just a city that reflects the diversity of the people that live in it, reflects its traditions and its history in all its institutions. I dream of a city that we should be inventing all the time, one that acts as a perpetual guide and initiator of the human spirit.

Indeed, a city is a place where the human destiny, the

great project of humanity unfolds. It is more than a home, a playground, a place of work. It is the new garden, the modern Eden, the open labyrinth. It is the instructor, the astonisher, the terrain of trial and reconciliation. It is the place where we plan, consciously or unconsciously, the redemption of humanity.

Here is the arena of the transformed journey from violence and selfishness and sundry evils, from hopelessness and loss of innocence to the future man and woman, people more at ease in the world, with a better history.

This is where we should dream a world where every individual can begin to realise their secret genius, their hidden happiness.

And how do we do this? By remembering that a city is a dream. It is a place of signs and hints and mysterious inscriptions. It is a living theatre of alchemical spaces that always whisper to the soul wherever it turns. And sometimes it whispers that here, in this world, in this life, there are fragments of paradise.

MUSINGS ON BEAUTY

Beauty is embraced truly by the soul. It has its roots deep in the subconscious. Its appeal is from deep down, in the hidden archetypes and the fundamental forms and the myths within that are but echoes of the stars.

Beauty is our sense of the mysteries of the universe. Beauty is always mysterious, because its true source is beyond reason. It belongs to higher causes rather than effects. But it is the effect of the higher origins of beauty's mystery that we experience as its reality.

We speak of the beauty of the moon when we are speaking not only of its pure round whiteness in the night sky, but also of the mysterious influence it exerts. We also imply its strange magnetism, its mesmeric hold on our imagination, and the inexplicable way it affects our bodies, our sleep, our moods, and all nature. When we gaze up at night the moon unifies our world-view. It is a mirror, reflecting the light of the sun, but in its own unique consistency.

The moon is more than what we see. Its appeal is cosmic and beyond the mind's full conscious comprehension. It is as deep in us as it is far above us. To see it is to resonate with a thousand invisible forces and feelings.

Such is beauty. To the religious it hints at the spiritual realm and draws the mind to a contemplation of the infinite. To the non-religious, it inspires fascination, pleasure, and desire. In both there is desire. In the spiritual, beauty inclines to desire for the highest, for the absolute. In literature it inclines towards an unquenchable hunger for the finest artistic impulses, for creativity, love. In the scientist, beauty inclines towards the great desire to understand, to explain, to make clear the laws of the universe, the mystery of all things – time, space, matter, light, creation.

Beauty leads us all, finally, to the greatest questions of all, to the most significant quest of our lives.

It is indeed a humbling thing that such a young poet,

touched by the sublime, could have given us, from notions already familiar to philosophers and mystics of the distant ages, the perfect formula, worthy of an Einstein or a Newton: 'Beauty is truth, truth beauty.'

Francis Bacon, who straddles the worlds of science and literature, put it wonderfully well when he wrote: 'The noblest use of the mind is the contemplation of the works of the creator.' If you probe the greatest achievements in literature or science or indeed any significant human endeavour you will find this to be more or less true.

The beauty of surfaces and the beauty of depths. Beauty in ugliness. Beauty in how time resolves evil. Beauty in birth and beauty in death. Beauty in the ordinary. Beauty in memory, in fading things, in forms perceived and not perceived.

Beauty in awkward, unfinished, ruined, broken things. Beauty in creation and in destruction. Beauty in time and in timelessness. Beauty in the infinite that encompasses all, before the beginning and beyond the end.

On Childhood (4)

1

Our childhoods pass obscure judgements on us. Looking at a picture of oneself as a child, who does not hear a faint whisper say: 'This is what you were; and look at who you have become'? We always let down the unstated promise inherent in our childhood. But we are not sure in what way. The failure eludes us somehow.

Childhood seems to promise so much, much that is unspecified. An eternal twinge of failure awaits the person who can meet, in spirit, the child that they were. For childhood seems to say that anything is possible, and that the golden ages can be incarnate in our time, within those lustrous eyes. And then the child becomes the person you are, here, now. Whoever you may be.

How fallen are the promises, how lowly are the glories!

Childhood is the enchanted judgement on the world, on society, and what we have let it become.

2

Childhood is the father and mother of humanity. In its mysterious estate lie our greatest secrets, our hopes, our redemption, the cures to our malaise.

3

Childhood is humanity's secret. If you want to understand a nation study the way it treats its children, the way it educates them, the way it moulds them. Study the children themselves.

Are they suspicious of the other? Then, for all their guises and civility, so are their parents. Then so is society. Are the children open to the other, to differences? Then more so are their parents, their society.

Children are the true thoughts of their nation, their class, their religion – the true thoughts untrammelled by diplomacy, politeness, politics, and hypocrisy.

Children betray the true nature of families. They reveal them. Or they redeem them. Children show what is good, what is true, what is pure, what is striven for, and what is natural in nations, and in families.

4

Childhood, paradoxically, is the future of all, not just its past. All great things incline us towards a higher childhood. Atlantis lives on in our imagination, and much can be learned from it. Eden has been transmuted into a future destination, made by our collective will and secret hopes, shaped by our hearts that yearn for a world where the unsuspected genius within us can live and unfold.

Childhood is the great puzzle, the marvellous symbol, the emblem of the quintessence, the magic mirror, the little grail, the missing key to our future.

5

This is why the childhood of literature is so important. Those early tales and fables can, at best, reveal to us our true, hidden, forgotten selves. It tells us who we are, and why. It dispels the shadows of the past. It shines a light on society. It brings back into our increasingly arid and closed minds the magic that dreams sometimes have. It makes some forgotten joy tremble in us. It makes us want to dream again, be free again, and to reach for childhood's elusive promise of a beautiful self. It makes us want to transform the world, and to be happy.

6

With the best writing about childhood something else happens. The world is made new. Fables become real. Reality becomes fabulous. Time and space are revealed as illusions. A vaster power flows through one's being. One senses that one can fly. For a magic moment all things are possible. Why not? The mind conceiving them makes them real. Childhood is about discovery. We rediscover the world, and are tempted to begin the grander journey of self-discovery. Then the closed circle becomes open again . . .

7

Novalis puts it beautifully. 'Where children are, there is a golden age.' Childhood is the golden age of humanity, invented in retrospect, with wonder woven in.

Through certain artists flows the childhood of the world, the forgotten angles, the golden ages of the spirit. In their best works we catch glimpses of the wondrous kingdom that childhood hints at. And we know that what we have glimpsed is not magic, or art, or enchantment. We know, in some obscure way, that the kingdom is real. This is what haunts us for ever.

O childhood, O initiation and birthplace of the world. You are the acorn, the seed, the ocean, the crossroads of past and future, the meeting place of lives; where what was is almost forgotten, and where what will be is seen 'as through a glass, darkly'.

> O childhood, elixir of time
> And of flowers;
> O childhood, where are those
> Lost, serene hours?

WHEN COLOURS RETURN
HOME TO LIGHT

1

The light came from the South, rose in the East, and flowered in the West. In the North it slumbers, and will awaken.

2

The god raped the girl, fertilised her consciousness with the bliss of origins, and named a continent.

3

These fragments are related.

4

Before the globe was split by the seas, all was one.

5

Then each fragment of the broken whole developed according to its special place in the universal scheme of secret destinies.

6

The myth of Europe is one, though many.

7

To understand. To dissect. To explain. To analyse. To prove. To make evident. To make practical.

8

Science is its religion, even in its religion.

9

Listen. A celebrated professor claims that Hamlet and his doubt, and his intellectual prosecution of reality, foreshadowed modern man and the plasma of the European self.

10

Frankenstein wanted to create, in the laboratory of science, the mystery of life – a living human being, from dead bodies and an electric spark. Culture would follow, it was presumed, from education and the environment. Frankenstein is a European, but so also is the monster.

11

Faust had exhausted all knowledge, secular and arcane, and explored the nebulous extremes of magic. The desire to know, the desire to master, seduces him into an immortal pact with Mephistopheles, a pact with his own soul, written in blood. Faust is European, but so also is Mephistopheles.

12

To know the impossible knowledge. To conquer unconquerable realms. To pierce the veil of the forbidden, the obscure. To use the mind and intellect as a laser. To prosecute the divine. This is the ideological DNA of the myth of Europe. These are the fragments. These are the original building blocks of the ruins.

13

Out of the myth of Europe has come as much good as evil. Fascism, the slave trade, and genocide have grown out of the need to master the forces of nature just as much as some of the world's greatest productions of art, the finest discoveries in science and governance. Civilisation, Western style, is the fruit of it, from the magnificent cathedrals, the Homeric epics, and the idealism of Plato to the ideas of democracy and all the attempts to achieve, by reason and power, a better life for its people. And the domination of the world.

14

The myth of Europe is the story of the light fertilising the intellect. The heart cries out in the myth.

15

Euripides heard that cry and elaborated, from the ancient rituals, the birth of Dionysus for the awakening of the European heart to the beautiful chaos of wine, to spiritual possession, to faith, to unknowing. The terror of the sublime must be encountered again.

16

This, it seems, was the warning that Euripides shaped: Do not deny the immeasurable mysteries. Surrender to the god that you cannot comprehend. Or great diseases of body and mind will invade your lives; and your conquests will be changed into the emptiness of the absurd; and you will dwell in the existential wastes of the spirit and the heart. You will dwell without wonder.

17

The origins of the Dionysian rituals are in the East and South, but they ought to penetrate the European myth. They ought to fertilise the myth, and lead the people towards an instinct for a new covenant.

18

The completion of a fragmented dream. The reunification of all humanity.

19

The myth of Europe is incomplete. It is the partial glimpse of what the mind sees and understands as it peers into the mirror of immortality. It catches glimpses of which its self is but a fragment, glimpses that can produce multiplication of knowledge, but ignorance of the infinite, of the one.

20

Europe is the only myth born from the divine that has ended in the murky text of unbelief. The brain's productions.

21

Its myth cries for feeling. Wagner knew this well. And music, at its most unmoored, sweeps the myth into realms where the head dare not go. For the whole edifice would crumble in the presence of such an examination.

22

The myth of Europe ought to return to its origin. To re-fertilise the bliss of the god into the heart and spirit. To re-create the original impact. To experience that joy for the first time.

23

So that the intellect may be illumined by the sublime hints of the shining jewel that dwells in us as the philosopher's stone, the ululations of Dionysus, the tranquillity of Apollo, the incarnation of Christ, and the whisperings of enigmatic wonderful dreams.

24

All our myths: they are needs refracted from our angle to the origin.

25

All our myths: they should be reunited in the knowledge that unless we return to the unfragmented truth of the family of humanity, unless we return love back to the centre of our ways, unless the colours return home to light, we will be trapped in our myths, which will then become our prisons. Then eventually will follow our doom, and the twilight of all our stories.

FORM AND CONTENT

Aphorisms

1

People think it is content which endures; but it is form which enables content to endure.

2

Form endures longer than content.

3

It is form that keeps content perpetually new and alive.

4

Form preserves the content like Greek vases or the Pyramids.

5

Everything has its own form. Every living thing has its living form.

6

The form unique to itself is what enables a thing to express its thingness. This is true of a fly, a particular short story, a painting or an individual.

7

Conforming to its generic type it is nonetheless unique to itself.

8

Nothing can live in art or in life that does not find the form unique to itself by which its individual soul can be expressed.

9

In that sense true form is both evanescent and eternal, a paradox, a mystery.

10

If something does not find its true form, it does not live.

11

Every true work of art is a meditation in form, and every meditation in form is a meditation on the mystery of life.

12

For the outer condition of life must correspond to the inner, and the outer condition of form must correspond to the inner condition of the work, its content, its dream, its spirit.

13

Form is the visible manifestation of spirit.

14

The spirit, infinitely greater than the form, shines through the form, as the soul shines through the body, or as the aura surrounds the body, pervades it, unseen to the eye, but sensed by the unacknowledged higher senses. It is this quality, this shining through, that makes a work of art greater than it seems.

15

As long as the form is capable of being a commensurate vehicle of spirit.

16

The medium is higher the more levels it has within it that correspond to the levels within us.

17

To find an invisible form.

18

Too much form means not enough spirit.

19

Too much spirit means not enough form.

20

To find the form that is also formless.

21

Or to find the formlessness which has form.

22

Whatever multiplies suggestiveness is best.

HEALING THE AFRICA WITHIN

1

Heart-shaped Africa is the feeling centre of the world.

2

Continents are metaphors.

3

A people are spiritual states of humanity as distinguishable in what they represent as roses, lions, and stars.

4

Have we forgotten what Africa is?

5

Africa is our dreamland, our spiritual homeland.

6

There is a realm in everyone that is Africa. We all have an Africa within.

7

When the Africa outside is sick with troubles, the Africa inside us makes us sick with neuroses.

8

The sheer quantity of inexplicable psychic illness in the world is possibly, indirectly, connected to the troubles in Africa.

9

We have to heal the Africa in us if we are going to be whole again.

10

We have to heal the Africa outside us if the human race is going to be at peace again in a new dynamic way.

11

There is a relationship between the troubles in a people and the troubles in the atmosphere of the world.

12

The troubles of Africa contribute immensely to the sheer weight and size of world suffering.

13

And this world suffering affects everyone on the planet, affects children and their health, affects our sleep, our anxiety, and our unknown suffering.

14

For it is possible to suffer without knowing it.

15

We have to heal the Africa within. We have to rediscover the true Africa. The Africa of laughter, of joy, of improvisation, and originality. The Africa of myths and legends, storytelling, and playfulness. The Africa of generosity, of hospitality, and compassion. The Africa of wisdom, mysticism, and divination. The Africa of paradox, proverbs, and surprise. The Africa of magic, faith, patience, and endurance. The Africa of a fourth-dimensional attitude to time. The Africa of a profound knowledge of nature's ways, and the secret cycles of destiny.

16

We have to rediscover Africa. The first encounter with Africa by Europe was the wrong one. It was not an encounter. It was an appropriation. What they saw, and bequeathed to future ages, was in fact a misperception. They did not see Africa. This wrong seeing of Africa is part of the problems of today. Africa was seen through greed and what could be got from it. This justified all kinds of injustice.

17

What you see is what you make. What you see in a people is what you eventually create in them.

18

It is now time for a new seeing. It is now time to clear the darkness from the eyes of the world.

19

The world should begin to see the light in Africa, its possibilities, its beauty, its genius.

20

If we see it, it will be revealed. We only see what we are prepared to see. Only what we see anew is revealed to us.

21

Africa has been waiting, for centuries, to be discovered with eyes of love, the eyes of a lover.

22

There is no true seeing without love.

23

We have to learn to love the Africa in us if humanity is going to begin to know true happiness on this earth.

24

We love the America in us. We love the Europe in us. The Asia in us we are beginning to respect. Only the Africa in us is unloved, unseen, unappreciated.

25

The first step towards the regeneration of humanity is making whole again all these great continents within us.

26

We are the sum total of humanity.

27

Every individual is all of humanity.

28

It is Africa's turn to smile.

29

That would be the loveliest gift of the twenty-first century: to make Africa smile again.

30

Then humanity can begin to think of the universe, even the remote stars, as its true home.

A TIME FOR NEW DREAMS

The crisis affecting the economy is a crisis of our civilisation. The values that we hold dear are the very same that got us to this point. The meltdown in the economy is a harsh symbol for the meltdown of some of our values. A house is on fire; we see flames coming through the windows on the second floor and we think that is where the fire is raging. In fact it is raging elsewhere.

For decades poets and artists have been crying in the wilderness about the wasteland, the debacle, the apocalypse. But apparent economic triumph has deafened us to these warnings. Now it is necessary to look at this crisis as a symptom of things gone wrong in our culture.

Individualism has been raised almost to a religion, appearance made more important than substance. Success justifies greed, and greed justifies indifference to fellow human beings. We thought that our actions affected only our own sphere, but the way that appalling financial decisions made in America have set off a domino effect makes it necessary to bring new ideas to the forefront of our civilisation. The most important is that we are more connected than we suspected. A visible and invisible mesh links economies and cultures around the globe to the great military and economic centres.

The only hope lies in a fundamental re-examination of the values that we have lived by in the past thirty years. It won't do just to improve the banking system – we need to redesign the whole edifice.

There ought to be great cries in the land, great anger. But there is a strange silence. Why? Because we are all implicated. We have drifted to this dark, unacceptable place together. We took the success of our economy as proof of the rightness of its underlying philosophy. We are now at a crossroads. Our future depends not on whether we get through this, but on how deeply and truthfully we examine its causes.

I strayed into the oldest church in Cheltenham not long ago

and, with no intention in mind, opened the Bible. The passage that met my eyes was from Genesis, about Joseph and the seven lean years of famine. Something struck me in that passage. It was the tranquillity of its writing, the absence of hysteria.

They got through because someone had a vision before the event. What we need now more than ever is a vision through and beyond the event, a vision of renewal.

As one looks over the landscape of contemporary history, one thing becomes very striking. The people to whom we have delegated decision-making in economic matters cannot be unaware of the consequences. Those whose decisions have led to the economic collapse reveal to us how profoundly lacking in vision they were. This is not surprising. They never were people of vision. They never had to be. They are capable of making decisions in the economic sphere, but how these decisions relate to the wider world was never part of their mental and ethical make-up. This is a great flaw of our world.

To whom do we turn for guidance? Teachers have had their scope limited by the prevailing fashions of education. Artists have become appreciated more for scandal than for important revelations about our lives. Writers are entertainers, provocateurs or – if truly serious – more or less ignored. The Church speaks with a broken voice. Politicians are guided by polls more than by vision. We have disembowelled our oracles. Anybody who claims to have a new vision is immediately suspect.

So now that we have taken a blowtorch to the ideas of sages, guides, bards, holy fools, seers, what is left in our cultural landscape? Scientific rationality has proven inadequate to the unpredictabilities of the times. It is enlightening that the Pharaoh would not have saved Egypt from its seven lean years with the best economic advisers to hand.

This is where we step out into a new space. What is missing

most in the landscape of our times is the sustaining power of myths that we can live by.

If we need a new vision for our times, what might it be? A vision that arises from necessity or one that orientates us towards a new future? I favour the latter. It is too late to react only from necessity. One of our much-neglected qualities is the creative ability to reshape our world. Our planet is under threat. We need a new one-planet thinking.

We must bring back into society a deeper sense of the purpose of living. The unhappiness in so many lives ought to tell us that success alone is not enough. Material success has brought us to a strange spiritual and moral bankruptcy.

If we look at the prevalence of alcoholism, the rise in suicides and our sensation addiction, we must conclude that the banishment of higher things from the garden has not been beneficial. The more society has succeeded, the more its heart has failed.

Everywhere parents are puzzled as to what to do with their children. Everywhere the children are puzzled as to what to do with themselves. The question everywhere is: you attain success, and then what?

We need a new social consciousness. The poor and the hungry need to be the focus of our economic and social responsibility.

Every society has a legend about a treasure that is lost. The message of the Fisher King is as true now as ever. Find the Grail that was lost. Find the values that were so crucial to the birth of our civilisation, but were lost in the intoxication of its triumphs.

We can enter a new future only by reconnecting what is best in us, and adapting it to our times. Education ought to be more global; we need to restore the pre-eminence of character over show, and wisdom over cleverness. We need to be more a people of the world.

All great cultures renew themselves by accepting the challenges of their times, and, like the biblical David, forge their vision and courage in the secret laboratory of the wild, wrestling with their demons and perfecting their character. We must transform ourselves, or perish.

And out of the wilderness
The songbird sang:

'Nothing is what it seems.
This is a time for new dreams.'

ACKNOWLEDGEMENTS

Material in this collection has been previously published as follows:

'On Childhood' in *Eye to Eye: Childhood* (New Internationalist Publications, 1998); 'Writers and Nations' in *Royal Society of Literature* Magazine, 2003; 'Plato's Dream' in *The Times Higher Education Supplement*, 2002; 'Photography and Immortality' in *BP Portrait Award 2009* (National Portrait Gallery, 2009); 'O, Ye who invest in Futures' in *The Caine Prize for Literature* (New Internationalist Publications, 2000); excerpt from 'Dramatic Moments in the Encounter between Picasso and African Art' in *Ode* Magazine, 2007; '10½ Inclinations' in *Royal Society of Literature* Magazine, 2006; 'Self-Censorship', the 2003 Scottish PEN Lecture at the Edinburgh International Book Festival, in the *Herald* (Glasgow), 2003; 'Healing the Africa Within' in *Ode* Magazine, 2004; and 'A Time for New Dreams' as 'A Time for New Values' in *The Times*, 2008.